D1144695

LONDON MIDLAND STEAM REVIVAL

Hugh Ballantyne

Copyright © Jane's Publishing Company Limited 1987

First published in the United Kingdom in 1987 by
Jane's Publishing Company Limited
238 City Road, London EC1V 2PU

ISBN 0 7106 0454 8

All rights reserved. No part of this publication may be
reproduced, stored in a retrieval system, transmitted in any
form by any means electrical, mechanical or photocopied,
recorded or otherwise without prior permission of the
publisher.

Printed in the United Kingdom
by Netherwood Dalton & Co Ltd, Huddersfield

JANE'S TRANSPORT PRESS

Cover illustrations

Front: 1986 saw Tyseley-based Class 5XP 'Jubilee' No 5593
Kolhapur make a welcome return to main line running, restored in
the splendid LMS passenger livery of maroon lined in black and
yellow. Here it is seen in the heart of LMS territory at Lostock
Junction near Bolton, hauling its second train of the day from
Manchester to Southport. 14 September 1986. *(Hugh Ballantyne)*
Leica M4-2   50mm f2 Summicron   Kodachrome 25   f2.8, 1/500

Back: Fowler-designed Class 7F 2-8-0 No 13809, one of a series of
five built by Robert Stephenson in 1925, returned to service in
1980 thanks to the efforts of the late Mr F Beaumont, after
withdrawal by BR as long ago as 1964. Designed for goods
working on the Somerset & Dorset Joint Railway, the 11 engines
of the class were frequently pressed into passenger service during
the 1950s and 1960s, so No 13809 looks quite at home seen
climbing past Kettlesbeck, east of Clapham, as she heads towards
Hellifield with the first leg of a 'Cumbrian Mountain Pullman'
train from Carnforth to Carlisle. 27 March 1982. *(Hugh
Ballantyne)*
Leica M4-2   50mm f2 Summicron   Kodachrome 25   f2, 1/500

Right: At the Severn Valley Railway's special weekend event of
June 1983 Stanier Class 5 No 5000 makes a most authentic sight at
the head of a goods as it comes off Victoria bridge and enters
Eymore Wood cutting on its way south towards Bewdley. 19 June
1983. *(David Eatwell)*
Canon AE-1   50mm FB f1.8   Kodachrome 64   f4, 1/500

Introduction

This is the second volume of 'Steam Revival' in the Publisher's 'Portfolio' series, and, as with my first book dealing with Great Western locomotives, the intention is to portray LMS-designed and LMS constituent company locomotives that have been restored to working order and have at some time or other been steamed since the 'Return to Steam' in 1971.

The London Midland & Scottish Railway was the largest of the four 'grouped' companies formed on 1 January 1923. It inherited by far the greatest number of engines, having approximately 10 400 as against 7700 of the next largest company, the LNER. At nationalisation on 1 January 1948 the LMS had about 8000 locomotives in service, so perhaps it is not surprising that LMS designs were used right up to the very end of BR steam operation in August 1968.

There are 100 LMS or constituent locomotives in existence in the United Kingdom, including the Liverpool & Manchester Railway trio of early locomotives. Excluding these three, *Rocket*, *Sans Pareil* and *Lion*, there are no less than 41 types represented, but three classes, comprising 18 Class 5s, 10 Fowler Class 3F 0-6-0Ts and seven Stanier Class 8Fs, make up over one-third of that total.

When one remembers the tremendous amount of physical effort required to restore and maintain these large items of reciprocating machinery by small numbers of skilful and tenacious people, with the work often undertaken in the most primitive of conditions, plus the cost in monetary terms, I think as enthusiasts we should all be truly grateful for what has been achieved. Not least, we should thank BR for allowing some of these locomotives to run from time to time.

Finally the Publishers and I would like to thank all the contributors, individually credited with their work, and who are all well known as being leading exponents of their art, for their unstinting co-operation and generosity in allowing me to include their photographs in this book.

HUGH BALLANTYNE
Eccleshall, North Staffordshire
March 1987

Below: Perhaps the locomotive type which epitomises LMS motive power in the eyes of many people is the ubiquitous Stanier Class 5 4-6-0. Not only were a total of 842 built, but as eminently successful mixed traffic engines they could be found all over the system from Bath in the south to Wick in the north. The first of the class entered service in 1934 and the last in 1951. Very much a standard class, there were a few variations to some of the locomotives built after 1947, and this picture shows one such example. Nos 4767 and 5407 are just coming off the north end of Ribblehead viaduct hauling a northbound 'Cumbrian Mountain Express'. The leading engine, built at Crewe in 1947, has outside Stephenson link motion and was the only one of the class so fitted, whilst the train engine, No 5407, built by Armstrong Whitworth of Newcastle upon Tyne in 1937, is an orthodox production unit with Walschaerts valve gear. 4 April 1981. *(Hugh Ballantyne)*
Leica M4-2   90mm Elmarit   Kodachrome 25   f4, 1/250

The handful of photographers who went to the Severn Valley Railway on this Saturday morning found the perfect winter photographic conditions very rarely seen in this country, with all the necessary ingredients obligingly falling into place on a steam operating day. First requisite is heavy snow fall, followed immediately by sub zero temperatures, no wind to blow the snow off the branches, and next morning high pressure to produce a sunny cloudless day! It was also a most commendable effort by the SVR volunteers and staff who kept the 'Santa Specials' running in these freezing conditions. Here is one of those trains hauled by Ivatt-designed Class 2F 2-6-0 No 46521 passing Northwood Farm en route to Bewdley with the thermometer reading −13°F. 12 December 1981.
(*Hugh Ballantyne*)
Leica M4-2   90mm Elmarit   Kodachrome 25

The first express passenger type produced by Mr W A Stanier for the LMS upon becoming its Chief Mechanical Engineer in 1932 was his Pacific 'Princess Royal' class, with the first two entering traffic in 1933 and the remaining 11 in 1935. These supremely elegant engines were later overshadowed by Stanier's 'Princess Coronation' Pacifics, of which a total of 38 were eventually built. Nevertheless these earlier Pacifics put in much good service on London, Liverpool and Glasgow express trains. Two have been preserved, the one shown here being No 6201 *Princess Elizabeth*, which following withdrawal by BR in 1962 was painstakingly restored by the Princess Elizabeth Locomotive Society at Ashchurch in Gloucestershire. She was later based at H P Bulmer Ltd, Hereford, and returned to main line working on 24 April 1976 with a run between Shrewsbury and Newport. The other locomotive, No 6203 *Princess Margaret Rose*, is on static display at the Midland Railway Centre, Butterley, Derbyshire. Here *Princess Elizabeth* heads south from Dorrington on the 1-in-90 rise towards Church Stretton with a 'Welsh Marches Express' on the second occasion this train ran. This subsequently became a popular steam special route between Chester and Newport. 14 February 1981. *(Hugh Ballantyne)*
Leica M4-2 50mm f2 Summicron
Kodachrome 25 f2-2.8, 1/500

LMS Class 7P No 6201 *Princess Elizabeth* again climbing a 1-in-90 gradient, this time in Lancashire between Lower Darwen and Darwen whilst hauling the 'Red Rose' bound for Shrewsbury from Carnforth. This engine had travelled north in early 1980 to work a number of specials from Carnforth, including the 'Cumbrian Mountain Express' on 8 July, and this train was organised to enable the 'Princess' to return to her base at Hereford. 27 September 1980. *(Hugh Ballantyne)*
Leica M4-2   50mm f2 Summicron
Kodachrome 25   f2, 1/500

Left: On a sunny spring afternoon the 'one off' Stephenson link motion Class 5 4-6-0 No 44767 looks most attractive in its BR lined black livery working hard to lift a 'Cumbrian Mountain Express' up the 1-in-100 climb west of Giggleswick as the train makes the second leg of its journey from Carlisle to Carnforth, the first section to Hellifield being hauled by BR Class 9F No 92220 *Evening Star.* 23 April 1984. *(Hugh Ballantyne)*
Leica M4-2   50mm f2 Summicron
Kodachrome 25   f2.8, 1/500

Above: By way of comparison with the Class 5 opposite, No 5305 has the usual Walschaerts valve gear and was one of 226 members of the class built by Armstrong Whitworth, in this case in 1937. It has been superbly restored in the pre-war LMS livery applicable to these engines, black lined in red. About this time the company was also putting into traffic some Class 5XP 4-6-0s painted in the impressive maroon livery reserved for express engines, and consequently these mixed traffic locomotives quickly became known as 'Black 5s', a

name which has stuck long after the passing of operational steam working. For additional effect the tyres have been burnished and this gives the engine a most attractive appearance. In this panned shot No 5305 is near Long Marton, north of Appleby, heading a southbound 'Cumbrian Mountain Express'. 29 December 1983. *(Hugh Ballantyne)*
Leica M4-2   50mm f2 Summicron
Kodachrome 25   f4-5.6, 1/60

This is the only preserved example of the last new locomotive type to be designed for the LMS, which was intended by the company to become one of its post-war standard classes. Designed by Mr H G Ivatt, these 2-6-0s were designated Class 4F and the first three entered service in the closing weeks of the independent LMS at the end of 1947. Eventually 162 of the type were built, the first 50 at Horwich and the remainder split between Doncaster, Darlington and Horwich. This engine, No 43106, was built at Darlington in 1951 and survived until June 1968, only two months before the elimination of steam from BR. It was bought for preservation on the SVR and arrived at Bridgnorth in August 1968, since when it has become a much liked and useful locomotive. In May 1974 it hauled the reopening train through from Bridgnorth to Bewdley and attended both the commemorative events referred to more fully on pages 12 and 13. On a bright autumn morning No 43106 climbs away from Bridgnorth with the 10.30 am train to Kidderminster. 21 October 1984.

(Hugh Ballantyne)
Leica M4-2   50mm Summicron
Kodachrome 25   f4, 1/250

The heavy goods locomotive introduced by Stanier in 1935 and classified 8F was to become another LMS post-war standard class. Eventually no less than 852 were constructed for use by the LMS, the War Department and Turkish State Railways, thus making them the largest Stanier-designed class (10 more than his Class 5). They were exceeded numerically by only three other types, the LNWR Class DX 0-6-0, GWR Class 57XX 0-6-0PT and 2-8-0 Austerity. Following the return of some of the WD engines to England after the Second World War, a total of 666 8Fs came into BR stock by 1957. Today just one or two remain on modest shed pilot duty in Turkey and five are preserved at home, two of which have been restored to operational service. These are No 8431, built at Swindon in 1944, which is on the KWVR (see page 58), and this engine, No 8233, built by North British in 1940, and saved by the Stanier 8F Locomotive Society following the end of steam in 1968 when it was withdrawn. It arrived at Bridgnorth in January 1969 and now sees regular use on the SVR. No 8233 can probably claim to be the most-travelled preserved locomotive in the country as it was built to Ministry of Supply order and entered service briefly on the LMS until 1941 when it was one of 51 8Fs requisitioned by the WD for service in Persia. In 1946 it went to Egypt and eventually came home to Longmoor in 1952. Following five years on the Military Railway it was sold to BR in 1957 and strangely given a new number, 48773, rather than its original No 8233. Now leading a more comfortable life in England's green and pleasant land, in contrast to that of harsh Middle Eastern deserts, No 8233 is seen making ready to leave Bridgnorth with the 12.20 pm train to Highley. 12 March 1977. *(Hugh Ballantyne)*
Leica M3   50mm f2 Summicron
Kodachrome 25   f8,1/60

A medium-size fast passenger 4-6-0 was introduced by Stanier in 1934, the same year as his mixed traffic Class 5 4-6-0, and somewhat similar in appearance save for driving wheels 9 in larger and the striking maroon livery applied to LMS express locomotives at the time. Classified 5XP, they became known as 'Jubilee' class because the first of the series, No 5552, was named *Silver Jubilee* in honour of King George V's Silver Jubilee in 1935. By 1936 a total of 191 engines had been built and they gave good service until the last was withdrawn in 1967. Four have been preserved, of which three have been restored to working order. This locomotive, No 5690 *Leander,* was built at Crewe in 1936 and withdrawn in 1964. Following preservation it was beautifully restored in the magnificent maroon livery and made its inaugural main line run on 1 September 1973. *Leander,* now owned by the SVR, has seen much main line running, and this picture and that opposite illustrate two of its many journeys.

Left: No 5690 accelerates hard out of Shrewsbury on the 1-in-127 rise towards Bayston Hill with a southbound 'Welsh Marches Pullman'. 13 March 1982.
(Hugh Ballantyne)
Leica M4-2   50mm f2 Summicron
Kodachrome 25   f2.5, 1/500

Right: On a cold winter's day No 5690 has traversed the points of the extensive track layout at Chinley North Junction (now simplified and reduced from four to two tracks) and is turning east towards Cowburn Tunnel and Edale with 'The Leander Envoy' train which it hauled from Guide Bridge to Carnforth. 24 February 1979. *(Hugh Ballantyne)*
Hasselblad FC2000
80mm f2.8 Planar
Agfa CT18   f3.5, 1/500

With the experience of Shildon behind them the organisers of 'Rocket 150', which was held at Rainhill in 1980 to commemorate the opening of the Liverpool & Manchester Railway in 1830, staged a cavalcade over the three days of the Spring Bank Holiday weekend. It was billed to have 40 participants and on the first day there were 37 entries of which 14 were LMS or constituent types. This picture shows LYR 0-6-0ST No 752 running as third entrant past the spectator stands; it is a saddle tank rebuild of the 0-6-0 type seen on page 35, which originated as a Barton Wright design but was rebuilt to the form seen here by Mr J A F Aspinall. This engine was built by Beyer, Peacock in 1881 and was sold out of service by the LMS to Blainscough Colliery at Coppull, Lancashire, in 1937. It became available for preservation in 1967, was rescued by the L&Y Saddle Tank Fund, and is now occasionally steamed on the KWVR. 24 May 1980.

(Hugh Ballantyne)
Leica M3   90mm f4 Elmarit
Kodachrome 25   f4, 1/250

Since the return to steam in 1971 there have been two major 150th anniversary events in which preserved steam has played the major role. The first was in 1975 to commemorate the opening of the Stockton & Darlington Railway in 1825. Staged as 'Rail 150' at Shildon, County Durham, it featured a cavalcade of locomotives to Heighington. The cavalcade only took place once and prior to the start the engines were prepared in the yard of Shildon Wagon Works. One of the smallest entries was this diminutive LYR 0-4-0ST No 51218, one of two of the class preserved, both on the KWVR. Fifty-seven of these small shunting engines were built, this one at Horwich in 1901 as No 68. It was the first locomotive preserved on the KWVR, arriving there as long ago as 1965, and in the 'Rail 150' event was one of 10 LMS or constituent engines out of 35 locomotives participating in the cavalcade. Behind it is *Fenchurch*, a small Stroudley-designed 0-6-0T for the LBSCR, which moved out into the cavalcade just after No 51218. 31 August 1975. *(Peter J C Skelton)*
Canon FTG 50mm
Kodachrome X f6.3, 1/250

Another LMS post-war type designated as a standard class was Ivatt's Class 2P 2-6-2T, first introduced in 1946. This was a tank version of the light Class 2F 2-6-0 illustrated on pages 3, 18, 30 and 64. The first was built at Crewe in 1946 and by 1952 130 had been constructed. Although mainly found on the London Midland Region, quite a number were also regularly used on the Southern and Western. This engine, No 41241, went new to Bath in 1949 and was mainly employed on local services to Bristol with occasional journeys down the Somerset & Dorset line. It was later transferred to Skipton. Following withdrawal in 1966 it was sold for preservation and went the short distance to its new home on the KWVR in 1967. Here it was repainted in red livery and lettered KWVR, and was used to haul (with 0-6-0T No 72) the inaugural train when the railway was reopened on 29 June 1968. In this picture, taken just after repainting in authentic BR lined black livery, this attractive and useful engine is seen on a bright spring afternoon piloting 0-6-0PT No L89 towards Ingrow station with a train up the valley to Oxenhope. 22 March 1980. (Hugh Ballantyne)
Leica M3   50mm f2 Summicron
Kodachrome 25   f2.8, 1/500

Another very large class which could be found all over the LMS system was the Class 4F 0-6-0 goods, of which no less than 772 were built. They originated on the Midland Railway as a Fowler design of 1911 and proved reliable in service. A total of 192 were constructed by the Midland, plus five by Armstrong Whitworth for the Somerset & Dorset in 1922. After grouping, the LMS had another 575 built between 1924 and 1941 in its own workshops and by contractors. Four have been preserved, but this engine, No 43924, is the only pre-grouping representative. It was bought from Woodham Bros scrapyard at Barry in 1968 by the Midland 4F Fund. It is in regular service on the KWVR, where it is seen acting as pilot to visiting Stanier Class 5 No 44767 working the 'Keighley Flyer', which the Class 5 had brought from Carlisle via the Settle & Carlisle line, over Mytholmes viaduct on the last stages of the journey to Oxenhope. 6 September 1986. (Hugh Ballantyne)
Leica M4-2   50mm f2 Summicron
Kodachrome 25   f2-2.8, 1/500

Most modern of the LMS express passenger fleet were the 38 Class 7P 'Princess Coronation' Pacifics designed by Stanier and built at Crewe between 1937 and 1948. Three are preserved but only this one, No 46229 *Duchess of Hamilton*, can be regarded as fully operational, and its restoration to service in May 1980 was a high water mark of railway preservation's return to steam. It has provided many memorable outings since, and these two pictures of it in action on the Settle & Carlisle route can only give a glimpse of the work it has performed.

Left: No 46229 gleams in the sun as it pounds upgrade at Sheriffs Brow between Settle and Horton-in-Ribblesdale with a northbound 'Cumbrian Mountain Express' to Carlisle (although displaying a 'Royal Scot' headboard), making its last outward run from its base at York prior to withdrawal for overhaul after nearly six years service. 19 October 1985. *(Peter J C Skelton)*
Yashica FRI 50mm ML
Kodachrome 64 f4.5, 1/500

Right: Many of the steam specials run in far from perfect weather and sometimes in atrocious conditions, but run they do all the year round, for which enthusiasts owe a great deal to the co-operation of BR and the various locomotive owners. On a dull and wet winter's day *Duchess of Hamilton* provides a magnificent sight working hard on the long 1-in-100 climb past Kirkby Stephen station towards Ais Gill summit with a southbound 'Cumbrian Mountain Express', this time displaying a 'Caledonian' headboard. 11 February 1984.
(Hugh Ballantyne)
Leica M4-2 90mm f2 Summicron
Kodachrome 64 f2, 1/500

Taken on the same December day as referred to on page 3, this picture emphasises the intense cold and wintry conditions prevailing in the loco stabling point at Bewdley with two of the SVR engines required to work the 'Santa Specials' to and from Arley, 2-6-0s No 46521 and 43106, raising steam. With the temperature at −13°F it was remarkable that the trains ran at all, but run they did, to the credit of the SVR and to the satisfaction of the customers who braved the cold that day for a trip out. 12 December 1981.
(Peter J C Skelton)
Hasselblad 500C/M   80mm
Ektachrome Pro 64   f11-16, 1/125

By contrast in weather and season, on a bright summer's morning an impressive line-up of SVR motive power was paraded outside Bridgnorth shed to provide a picture as good as and reminiscent of some of the pre-war publicity pictures of the main line companies showing their top link locomotives 'Ready for the Road'. In this line-up the locomotives are, from left to right, BR Class 4 2-6-4T No 80079, Class 5 No 5000, Class 4F No 43106, Class 2F No 46443 and Longmoor Military Railway No 600 *Gordon*. Although the nearest and furthest engines are not of LMS lineage, the influence of that company can clearly be seen in the BR Standard Class 4 2-6-4T which was a development of the well-proven LMS Fairburn and Stanier engines of similar type and illustrated on pages 28 and 29. 13 September 1981.
(D C Williams)
Pentax SP500   Kodachrome 64   f6.3, 1/125

Thanks to the initiative and co-operation of BR Scottish Region, steam power returned to the 42-mile Mallaig extension of the West Highland line in May 1984. This picture not only portrays the historic return to steam after 22 years absence, but shows some of the magnificent scenery to be found in that part of Scotland. Here Stanier Class 5 No 5407, built by Armstrong Whitworth in 1937, comes steadily around the curves at the western end of Loch Eilt as it nears Lochailort station on the first weekend journey from Fort William. To add to the occasion, the locality enjoyed beautiful sunny weather over the entire weekend, which was the Spring Bank Holiday, whilst the rest of the British Isles including most of Scotland suffered continuous heavy rain! 28 May 1984. *(John Laverick)*
Mamiya 645   80mm Sekor
Agfa R100S   f5.6, 1/500

The longest viaduct on the Fort William to Mallaig line is to the east of Glenfinnan station, where the railway curves around to cross the base of the glen and over the River Finna, near where the river seeks its outlet into Loch Shiel. Like most other viaducts on the Mallaig extension, it was built with concrete, which at the time was an innovation, by the contractor Robert McAlpine. The viaduct has 21 spans of 50 ft, with a total length of 1248 ft and maximum height of 100 ft on a curve of 12 chains radius. The photograph also portrays the fine scenery to be found in the West Highlands as Class 5 No 44767 *George Stephenson* heads westwards steadily across the viaduct with a train to Mallaig. 4 August 1986. *(Geoffrey Dingle)*
Mamiya 645 1000S   Fujichrome 100
f5.6, 1/500

A fine individual effort by one man, Mr F Beaumont, and his small team of expert helpers privately restored 2-8-0 Class 7F No 13809 from Barry scrapyard condition to BR running order, and in 1980 this ex-Somerset & Dorset Joint Railway goods engine returned to main line running. It ran from Guide Bridge to York via Sheffield, and for this job was given facilities at the Dinting Railway Centre. Here it is seen crossing Dinting viaduct running light engine to Guide Bridge to pick up its first train. The engine was one of five built by Robert Stephenson in 1925 to supplement six earlier locomotives built at Derby in 1914. It became SDJR No 89, and in common with the rest of the class spent its entire working life at Bath on S&D trains and also working to Bristol, Avonmouth and Gloucester. It was withdrawn in 1964 and sent to Barry for scrap. 2 May 1980. *(Hugh Ballantyne)*

Leica M3   50mm f2 Summicron
Kodachrome 25   f4-5.6, 1/250

Steam locomotives always look impressive at night and none more so than in this picture of Class 7F 2-8-0 No 13809 standing in the platform at Sheffield with its oil-fed lamps piercing into the darkness. On this occasion No 13809 was returning to its base at Butterley having earlier in the day worked the Carnforth to Hellifield section of a 'Cumbrian Mountain Pullman' train. There is a second SDJR 2-8-0, No 13808, preserved; rescued from Barry in 1970, it is still undergoing long-term restoration on the West Somerset Railway at Watchet. 2 May 1983. (L A Nixon)
Nikon F   85mm Nikkor
Kodachrome 25   f5.6, 20 sec

23

Left: Regarded by many as the finest express passenger locomotive type built in this country, Stanier's 'Princess Coronation' class Pacific No 46229 *Duchess of Hamilton* pulls away from Northwich station as it sets out for York with the 'Hadrian Pullman'. 18 July 1981.
(Hugh Ballantyne)
Leica M4-2   50mm f2 Summicron

Kodachrome 25   f2-2.8, 1/500

Below: After spending two weeks in Herefordshire during its only visit to the border counties up to the present time, No 46229 *Duchess of Hamilton* returned by night to York, with the two Club 55 Pullmans *Eagle* and *Emerald* and Royal brake No 5155, having earlier hauled the 'Welsh Marches Pullman' northwards to Chester. The photographer, living locally, was fortunately on hand to make this interesting flash-light shot as the train came through Altrincham station. 6 November 1982.
(Keith Sanders)
Nikon FE   50mm Nikkor   Ektachrome 200 f4 with Vivitar 365 flash, 1/125

Class 5 No 44932, built at Horwich in 1945, looks very smart in BR lined black livery with the early full lettering on the tender as it nears Banavie with an SRPS rail tour, steam hauled from Fort William to Mallaig. In the background part of Ben Nevis can be seen, which at 4406 ft is the highest mountain in Great Britain. 30 August 1986. *(John Kenward)*

Canon AE-1 Program   Kodachrome 64
f3.5, 1/250

A golden Class 5, transformed by the evening sun reflecting off No 44932, seen at Fort William on the same day as the picture opposite. Since 1984, when steam returned to the Mallaig extension, two Class 5s have been based at Fort William each season to work the services and 1986 was the first year this Carnforth-based engine came north to share the work with No 44767. For the first two seasons Carnforth's participant had been No 5407, which had the honour of working the inaugural train in May 1984. 30 August 1986.
(Keith Sanders)
Nikon FE   50mm Nikkor
Fujichrome 100   f16, 1/30

On 2 May 1973 the Lakeside & Haverthwaite Railway reopened part of the former Furness Railway branch originally opened in 1869 between Plumpton Junction near Ulverston and Lakeside, situated at the south end of Windermere, a distance of 8 miles. The branch was closed to passengers by BR on 6 September 1965 and to goods traffic in April 1967. After this the preservation company negotiated to purchase 3½ miles of the branch from Haverthwaite, as expensive roadworks necessary south of that station made purchase of the whole branch impracticable at the time. The new owners have fortuitously been able to preserve two of the once-extensive fleet of 645 LMS 2-6-4Ts, in the form of Fairburn-designed Nos 42073 and 42085 built after nationalisation at Brighton in 1950 and 1951 respectively. In addition the railway has the benefit of a fine terminus station with convenient connection facilities for the lake steamer services. This picture, taken in the first operating season, shows Class 4P 2-6-4T, renumbered 2073 and painted black lined red, coming into Lakeside station with the 4.25 pm train, the formation of which presents a uniformly smart appearance with a set of BR Mk1 coaches. 16 July 1973. (*Hugh Ballantyne*)
Leica M3   50mm Summicron
Agfa CT18   f4, 1/250

The LMS, as the largest UK railway company, was a prolific user of big Class 4P 2-6-4Ts on its many suburban train services and cross-country routes, and following Fowler's 125 engines put in traffic between 1927 and 1934 his successor, W A Stanier, produced in 1934 a taper boiler series of 2-6-4T with three cylinders for service on the London Tilbury & Southend section. A total of 37 were built, all at Derby, and he followed these up with another 206 of similar appearance but with two cylinders. Stanier's first 2-6-4T, No 2500, withdrawn in 1962, has been preserved as part of the national collection and for many years has been in the care of Alan Bloom's Bressingham Gardens Centre in Norfolk, together with other BR engines including LTSR 4-4-2T No 80 *Thundersley*, No 6100 *Royal Scot* and No 6233 *Duchess of Sutherland*. No 2500 repainted in original livery looks a most impressive sight on one of the rare occasions it has been seen in steam at Bressingham. 15 August 1976.
(Derek Smith)
Pentax SP500   50mm f2 Takumar
Kodachrome 25   f5.6, 1/125

Left: A pleasing sight on the SVR for the 1986 Enthusiasts' Weekend event was the double-heading of the 11.25 am Bridgnorth to Kidderminster train with two of the LMS standard classes, Ivatt-designed Mogul No 46443 piloting No 43106 southwards out of Bewdley. The bare land in the left foreground had recently been cleared by contractors building the Bewdley by-pass, for future use by the railway as sidings. Two months after the picture was taken a section of embankment seen at the tail of the train was removed and a pre-cast concrete bridge placed into position; so the railway now spans new by-passes at both Bridgnorth and Bewdley. 20 September 1986.
(Geoffrey Dingle)
Mamiya 645 1000S
Fujichrome 100 f5.6, 1/500

Right: As is usual at SVR special weekend events, the railway creates a great deal of interest by running demonstration goods trains. During the Summer Gala Weekend of 1984 Fowler-designed Class 3F 0-6-0T No 47383, built by Vulcan Foundry in 1926 and withdrawn by BR in 1967, comes south near Northwood Farm with a Highley to Bewdley goods. Some 442 of these 0-6-0Ts were constructed between 1924 and 1931, all by contractors except the last 15 which were turned out from Horwich Works in 1931. They supplemented 60 engines of similar type previously built by the Midland Railway, and despite their vintage origin were sufficiently well-regarded by the LMS to be designated as one of the post-war standard classes. Ten locomotives from this large class avoided cutting up and are now all owned by preservationists. 24 June 1984.
(John Laverick)
Mamiya 645   80mm Sekor
Agfa CT18   f4, 1/500

Left: Contrast by night at Dinting Railway Centre near Glossop. This location is the home of both engines shown, 'Converted Royal Scot' No 6115 *Scots Guardsman* and LNWR 0-6-2T Coal Tank No 1054. Both engines have seen service on BR approved routes although No 6115, an LMS express passenger locomotive, regrettably made only a few runs in 1978 and has since been mostly confined to its home base, a severe restriction for such a powerful Class 6P 4-6-0. By comparison the little Coal Tank in 1984 and 1986 attracted a great deal of attention and goodwill by visits to Manchester and to the KWVR and SVR, topped-off by a birthday special for octogenarian enthusiast Mr W A Camwell from Shrewsbury to Stockport via Chester in October 1986. 3 August 1986. *(Brian Dobbs)*
Mamiya 645   80mm Sekor
Fuji RDP 100   f5.6, 30 secs

Right: To alleviate the critical express passenger locomotive shortage the LMS was facing shortly after the grouping in 1923, Sir Henry Fowler in conjunction with North British Loco Co designed a powerful 4-6-0 type resulting in 50 engines built by the contractors in 1927 to become the 'Royal Scot' class. Compared with the then existing power, these locomotives were a godsend to the Operating Department and Derby Works constructed another 20 in 1930. The 'Royal Scots' provided the mainstay of express passenger power for all the Anglo-Scottish expresses and services to north-west England, and were only gradually superseded on the heaviest trains in later years by Stanier Pacifics. In 1943 Sir William Stanier converted No 6103 *Royal Scots Fusilier* with his No 2A taper boiler, and the whole class was so dealt with by 1955. The converted engines plus similarly rebuilt 'Patriots' and two 'Jubilees' were power Class 6P and designated a standard class. All the 'Converted Royal Scots' were withdrawn by 1965 but two survive, and except for very limited running by No 6115, referred to above, neither locomotive sees active line service. No 6100 *Royal Scot* is at Bressingham Gardens, Norfolk, while No 6115 is at Dinting. Seen here, No 6115 *Scots Guardsman* looks in fine form in LMS post-war passenger livery of black lined in maroon and straw as it climbs into Buxworth cutting on the early stages of its journey with the 'Yorkshire Venturer' train from Guide Bridge to York. 11 November 1978.
(Hugh Ballantyne)
Hasselblad 2000FC   80mm f2.8 Planar
Agfa CT18   f4, 1/500

The Lancashire &
Yorkshire Railway, a very
workmanlike and relatively
compact system, which was
amalgamated with the
LNWR two years before
the Grouping, used plain
conventional engines and
relied heavily on various
0-6-0 types that carried out
prodigious amounts of
hard work. This is a
representative locomotive
from that railway, now
preserved at Carnforth,
and was one of 448 engines
built to the design of John
Aspinall between 1889 and
1917. This engine, LYR
No 1300, built at Horwich
in 1896, ended up as BR
No 52322; it was
withdrawn in 1960 and
then sold to Leonard
Fairclough & Co, civil
engineers of Adlington,
Chorley. It is seen at
Carnforth shortly after it
had been repainted in LYR
passenger livery, black
lined with red and white.
Behind it stands industrial
0-6-0ST *Lindsay*. 29 May
1982. *(Hugh Ballantyne)*
Hasselblad 2000FC
80mm f2.8 Planar
Agfa CT18   f8-11, 1/60

On a bright blustery day a KWVR double-headed train from Keighley is hauled by ex-LYR Class 2F 0-6-0 No 52044 piloting Ivatt Class 2P 2-6-2T No 41241 into Damems loop. No 52044 is a Barton Wright-designed goods engine and was built by Beyer, Peacock in 1887. It was withdrawn by BR in June 1959 and afterwards became one of the earliest standard-gauge locomotives privately preserved when it was purchased by Mr A Cox who kept it at Retford. The engine came to the KWVR in 1965 and was later painted in a fictitious livery and used in making a film 'The Railway Children'. Following this it was repainted back into authentic BR plain black livery and has made occasional appearances in steam on its home railway, as seen here. 22 March 1975. *(G W Morrison)*
Pentax S1A   Kodachrome 25   f3.5, 1/250

35

Easily the oldest original working locomotive in this country, and second oldest in the world, is Liverpool & Manchester Railway 0-4-2 *Lion* owned by Merseyside County Council. This priceless piece of early locomotive engineering was built by Todd Kitson & Laird of Leeds in 1838 and withdrawn as long ago as 1857, by which time it had become LNWR No 116. The LNWR sold it for £400 in 1859 to Mersey Docks & Harbour Board for use as a stationary pumping engine at Prince's Dry Dock, Liverpool. In 1928 the engine was donated to Liverpool Engineering Society, and afterwards the LMS carried out repairs to the locomotive at Crewe Works to enable it to steam at the Liverpool & Manchester Railway centenary celebrations in 1930. *Lion* then went back into honourable retirement on a pedestal at Liverpool Lime Street station, but later became a film star when it was back in steam in 1953 for the making of the Ealing Studios comedy 'The Titfield Thunderbolt' filmed on the then recently closed Limpley Stoke to Camerton branch near Bath. In 1979 it went to Vulcan Foundry at Newton-le-Willows (by then known as Ruston Diesels Ltd) where it was thoroughly overhauled in time to appear at the 150th anniversary of the LMR at Rainhill in May 1980 (see page 12). Between overhaul and the Rainhill event the engine was kept at Steamport, Southport, and this picture shows *Lion* leaving Burscough en route from Wigan to Southport following renovation. 24 March 1980. *(Hugh Ballantyne)*
Leica M3   50mm f2 Summicron
Kodachrome 25   f4, 1/250

Another classic LMS constituent engine, and regarded by many as the ultimate in elegant English locomotive design of the Victorian era, was S W Johnson's Class 1P single-wheeler of which 95, known as 'Spinners', were built between 1887 and 1900. This engine subsequently became No 673 and was withdrawn in 1928 after which it was preserved by the LMS with its original number 118. It is now kept at the Midland Railway Trust at Butterley, and not surprisingly this beautiful locomotive was selected to appear in 'Rocket 150' at Rainhill. Following this event No 673 and Class 4F No 4027, also housed at Butterley, appeared at Tinsley depot open day on 15 June 1980, and in the evening the pair made their way home. They are seen during that journey near Chesterfield. 15 June 1980.
(L A Nixon)
Nikon F   85mm Nikkor
Kodachrome 25   f2, 1/250

Below: A rare one-off survivor from a class of 280 Midland Railway Johnson-designed Class 1F 0-6-0Ts is No 1708 seen at work on the KWVR where it was based before moving to the Midland Railway Trust at Butterley. These small shunting engines were built between 1874 and 1899 with open-backed cabs, although some were later fitted with all-over cabs. No 1708 was built in 1880 and withdrawn in 1966, following which it was bought and sent to Haworth for preservation. In this picture No 1708 pilots Class 2P No 41241 at milepost 4¼ south of Haworth as they climb towards the terminus at Oxenhope on a lovely spring afternoon. 18 April 1971. *(G W Morrison)*
Pentax S1A   Kodachrome 25   f3.5, 1/250

Right: This picture gives an authentic atmosphere to the KWVR as a former Midland Railway branch line showing Fowler Class 4F No 43924 coming through the woods towards Oxenhope with a train of BR non-corridor coaches. 29 December 1985. *(Geoffrey Dingle)*
Mamiya 645 1000S   Fujichrome 100   f5.6, 1/500

The Llangollen Railway was until recently a relatively unknown organisation, but has been making progress steadily and using to best advantage its beautiful situation in the Dee valley and the substantial GWR station at Llangollen. The major breakthrough came in 1986 when the line was extended to Berwyn, a distance of 1½ miles, in a delightful location alongside the river. Not surprisingly and most encouragingly the railway has now seen an increase in passengers and receipts and eventually it hopes to extend its tracks to Carrog. The only ex-BR engine in service at present is LMS Class 3F 0-6-0T No 7298, built by Hunslet in 1924 and withdrawn in 1966, which is seen leaving Llangollen station with the 3.00 pm train to Berwyn. 24 August 1986. *(Hugh Ballantyne)*
Leica M4-2   50mm f2 Summicron
Kodachrome 25   f2-2.8, 1/500

The Midland Railway Trust at Butterley in Derbyshire has four of the 10 preserved LMS Class 3F 0-6-0Ts, of which No 16440 has been put back into traffic. It was built by North British in 1926, later became BR No 47357 and was eventually withdrawn in 1966. It is restored with its original LMS number but repainted in maroon rather than the correct but less spectacular black which was its only livery in LMS/BR ownership. Here the little Class 3F pilots No 4027, the first LMS Class 4F 0-6-0 built at Derby in 1924, over the embankment at Hammersmith with a train to Ironville during the MRT enthusiasts' weekend of 1982. 3 October 1982. *(Hugh Ballantyne)*

Hasselblad 2000FC   80mm f2.8 Planar
Agfa CT18   f4, 1/500

The SVR has two Stanier Class 5s in its care, No 5000 (see page 1) which is part of the national collection, and this engine No 45110 which was purchased by the company in the year the picture was taken. No 45110 was built by Vulcan Foundry in 1935 and from new spent most of its life allocated to Holyhead shed. In the last years of BR steam it was transferred to Stafford in 1964 and from 1965 to 1968 was at Bolton and Lostock Hall, Preston. Its main claim to fame is that it hauled BR's last steam train on 11 August 1968 from Liverpool Lime Street to Carlisle as far as Manchester Victoria. Following this it was purchased, and eventually came to the SVR in August 1970, commencing work shortly afterwards. Later it was named *RAF Biggin Hill* and is seen so named and in BR lined black livery on a spring day climbing Eardington bank with the 4.40 pm from Highley to Bridgnorth, comprising a very mixed rake of stock. 16 April 1974.
(Hugh Ballantyne)
Leica M3   50mm f2 Summicron
Kodachrome II   f4, 1/250

When H G Ivatt's last design of locomotive for the LMS, the Class 4F 2-6-0 standard class, was first produced its appearance caused something of a culture shock to enthusiasts who were (with the one exception of the Bulleid Q1) quite unused to seeing fully-exposed driving wheels, high running plate, visible pipework and a high-pitched cab on British-designed locomotives! Time has mellowed attitudes and No 43106, the only survivor of the 162-strong class, has become a much-liked engine on the SVR where it is seen in this panned shot near Eardington working a Highley to Bridgnorth train. 16 April 1974. *(Hugh Ballantyne)*
Leica M3   50mm f2 Summicron
Kodachrome II   f8-11, 1/30

One unique preserved locomotive in the national collection is Midland Railway Compound Class 4P 4-4-0 No 1000, the first of 45 engines designed by Johnson and built between 1902 and 1909. They were substantially rebuilt by Fowler with superheated G9AS boilers which completely transformed their appearance to that visible in these pictures. Following dynamometer car trials in 1923 by the then newly-formed LMS between a Compound and an LNWR 'Prince of Wales' 4-6-0 on the Settle & Carlisle line, the former was found to have more economical coal consumption and greater ability to handle heavy trains over severely graded lines. The LMS went on to build a further 195 Compounds between 1924 and 1932. For a while these locomotives penetrated many parts of the system and worked important express passenger trains. Not surprisingly perhaps, they received a poor reception on the former LNWR section, where the men were used to hard driving and working simple expansion engines with long cut-offs and regulators only partly open, to which treatment the Compounds did not take kindly. However, they established a fine reputation on many routes, notably the Midland main line, Leeds–Morecambe residential trains, and on the Glasgow & South Western. Gradually the construction of more Stanier 4-6-0s from 1934, and later the 2-6-4Ts, led to a decline in duties for the Compounds, and the original MR series was withdrawn between 1948 and 1952 whilst the LMS batch lasted until 1961. No 1000 was withdrawn in 1951. Fortunately BR decided to renovate it and return it to limited traffic use in 1959 as MR No 1000 in its superheated condition and the full glory of Midland red livery. *Below:* No 1000 comes across the River Nidd viaduct at Knaresborough with a private charter from York to Leeds via Harrogate and back to York. 7 October 1981. *(David C Rodgers)*
Pentax MX 50mm Takumar Kodachrome 25 f3.8, 1/250
Right: Class 4P Compound No 1000 looks a splendid sight as it comes out of Marsh Lane cutting at Leeds with the same private charter train. 7 October 1981. *(G W Morrison)*
Pentax S1A Kodachrome 25 f3.5, 1/250

Sadly the largest constituent company of the LMS, the London & North Western Railway, has not had many of its locomotives preserved. This is probably because most of its better known main line classes were withdrawn in the 1930-40s, when preservation of locomotives was not really regarded as a matter of national importance but done merely at the whim of the owning railway company and without much outside influence being exerted. However the LMS did preserve some interesting LNWR engines and two have been seen at work since the 1971 steam revival. Above is 'Jumbo' 2-4-0 No 790 *Hardwicke* built at Crewe in 1892, a renewal of an earlier 'Precedent' class engine built in 1873. In its later form it became famous in the summer of 1895 during the railway races from London to Aberdeen when it covered the 141 miles between Crewe and Carlisle in 126 minutes at an average speed of 62.4 mph, albeit with a very light train. After withdrawal in 1932 the LMS preserved it and No 790 is now part of the national collection. It has made occasional outings on to BR and is seen here piloting Compound No 1000 out of Weeton Tunnel on a journey from York to Leeds and Carnforth for the Gainsborough Model Railway Society. Despite the ugly and over-prominent headboard, this historic pair of locomotives make a most impressive sight. 24 April 1976. (*G W Morrison*)
Pentax S1A   Kodachrome 25   f3.5, 1/250

Stanier Class 5 No 5305 (now named *Alderman A E Draper* after the gentleman whose firm purchased it from BR) heads northwards out of Blea Moor Tunnel into a most welcome patch of sunlight on a winter's morning. It was hauling a special train organised by West Yorkshire County Council to publicise the public enquiry which was due to start at Appleby two weeks later about the future of the Settle & Carlisle line. 8 March 1986.

(Hugh Ballantyne)
Leica M4-2   90mm f2 Summicron
Kodachrome 25   f2, 1/500

47

The sleek Stanier Pacific No 6201 *Princess Elizabeth* made a welcome return to service after a four-year overhaul at Hereford, and performed its first revenue run from Stockport to Carnforth via Leeds in 1986. The autumn day was fine and here the elegant Pacific is caught in the glow of the late-afternoon sunshine as she tackles the climb towards Giggleswick station and the summit beyond during the later stages of the journey. 15 November 1986.

(Geoffrey Dingle)
Mamiya 645 1000S
Fujichrome 100   f4-5.6, 1/500

Jubilee Class 5XP No 5690 *Leander* still has steam to spare as she comes fast through Reddish station on the former LNWR line from Heaton Norris Junction, Stockport, to Stalybridge via Guide Bridge, heading an eastbound 'Trans Pennine Pullman' from Northwich to Leeds. 10 April 1982.

(Hugh Ballantyne)
Leica M4-2   50mm f2 Summicron
Kodachrome 25   f2.2, 1/500

Left: A dramatic picture, taken at just the right moment to emphasise the reflection, of Class 5 No 44932 crossing the bridge over the River Lochy near Fort William on its return journey from Mallaig. 30 August 1986.
(John Kenward)
Canon AE-1 Program

Kodachrome 64   f8, 1/500

Above: No 44767 *George Stephenson* looks in good fettle as it sets out from Fort William with the 11.10 am train to Mallaig during the first season of steam's return to this spectacular line. So far two Stanier Class 5 locomotives have been required to cover each season's operations and this engine shared the work with No 5407 during 1984. 19 July 1984.
(Geoffrey Dingle)
Mamiya 645 1000S
Fujichrome 100   f5.6, 1/500

The SRPS operates a short railway in West Lothian called the Bo'ness & Kinneil Railway and is actively engaged in extending its line to Birkhill and improving facilities, not least of which has been the reconstruction of the former Edinburgh Haymarket trainshed to create this impressive station at Bo'ness. The station also has (bottled) gas lighting to enhance its period atmosphere. The railway has one ex-BR engine at work, one of the few Caledonian Railway engines preserved. It is a J F McIntosh-designed 439 class 0-4-4T No 419 which later became LMS Class 2P

No 15189. It was one of 68 built between 1900 and 1914, this locomotive appearing from St Rollox Works in 1907. It became the sole survivor, finally working at Carstairs until it was included in the huge number of Scottish Region locomotive withdrawals of December 1962. Now restored in the splendid Caledonian passenger livery of Prussian blue lined out with black bands edged on both sides with a white line, and footplate facings and steps crimson lake, you can clearly see the attractive appearance No 419 presents. Note also the additional embellishments of thistles on the

wing plates and star around the smokebox door handle as No 419 prepares to leave Bo'ness with its train for Kinneil. 6 April 1986.
(Roger Siviter)
Nikon FM   50mm f2 Nikkor
Kodachrome 64   f5.6, 1/250

Right: No 419 brings a train from Kinneil along the foreshore of the Firth of Forth as it heads towards Bo'ness. 6 April 1986.
(Roger K Hill)
Canon AE-1 Program   50mm
Ektachrome 100   f8, 1/250

Above: Stanier Class 5 No 5305 *Alderman A E Draper* makes a fine picture appropriately heading a 'Santa' steam express through the snow-covered countryside north-west of Bempton on the single line section between Bridlington and Seamer Junction with a train which had started from King's Cross. No 5305 worked the train between Hull and Scar-

borough. 28 December 1985. *(David Peaker)*
Mamiya 645   80mm Sekor
Ektachrome 100   f2.8, 1/500

Right: A highlight of 1983 BR steam running was the double-headed combination of two engines in maroon livery, an impressive pairing of locomotives which is visually hard to

beat. Despite the overcast conditions of a midwinter's day, the sight of Midland Compound No 1000 piloting Class 5XP 'Jubilee' No 5690 *Leander* very near the top of the long 1-in-100 climb to Ais Gill summit with a southbound 'Cumbrian Mountain Pullman' was well worth the effort. 12 February 1983. *(Peter Millar)*
Mamiya 645   150mm Sekor

The North London Railway was taken over by the LNWR as long ago as 1909. It was a small local company with only two main classes of locomotive, a distinctive 4-4-0T for passenger work and the 0-6-0T type seen here for goods and shunting, so we are most fortunate that one of the 0-6-0Ts has been preserved. Thirty engines were designed by J C Park in 1879 and this one was built at Bow Works in 1880 as NLR No 76. It later became LNWR No 2650 and much later on BR was Class 2F No 58850. In the meantime it left its native London haunts for a rural life on the Cromford & High Peak line in Derbyshire and gave good service on this freight only railway until, as the last survivor of the class, it was withdrawn in 1960. Following purchase it went back to the south of England and arrived on the Bluebell Railway in 1962. Although little used except for hiring to contractors for demolition train work on the East Grinstead line in 1964-65, it returned to service in 1984 after long overhaul, in BR No 58850 livery. It is very pleasing to see this powerful little engine working again, and this picture shows it hauling a train away from Freshfield Halt towards Sheffield Park. Note the GNR observation car next to the engine. 7 September 1986. *(Michael Esau)*
Rolleiflex f3.5 Fujichrome 100

Besides *Hardwicke* (see page 46) the other active LNWR locomotive is this little F W Webb Coal Tank 0-6-2T No 1054. One of 300, it was built at Crewe in 1888 and eventually became Class 2F No 58926. Following withdrawal it came into the ownership of the National Trust and is currently based at Dinting Railway Centre. In 1980 it took part in 'Rocket 150' at Rainhill and made other appearances as referred to on page 32. In 1986 it visited the SVR before working Mr W A Camwell's birthday special to Stockport, and proved a great attraction on the SVR where it is seen passing Bewdley South signalbox with the 10.00 am train from Bridgnorth to Kidderminster. 20 September 1986. *(Hugh Ballantyne)*
Leica M4-2   50mm f2 Summicron
Kodachrome 25   f2-2.8, 1/500

57

Above: LMS goods engines ready for the day's work standing in the yard at Haworth, KWVR: Class 8F No 8431, built at Swindon in 1944 and 0-6-0 Class 4F No 43924 built at Derby in 1920. 6 September 1981. *(Hugh Ballantyne)*
Leica M4-2   50mm f2 Summicron
Kodachrome 25   f4, 1/60

Right: Super power on the KWVR as two contractor-built Stanier Class 5s No 45212 (Armstrong Whitworth 1935) pilots No 5025 (Vulcan Foundry 1934) up-grade out of Keighley station as they set out with a train to Oxenhope. No 5025 was subsequently transferred north and is now resident on the Strath-

spey Railway, since when it has made some BR runs from Perth to Aviemore and on the Inverness to Kyle of Lochalsh line. 17 March 1973.
(G W Morrison)
Pentax S1A   Kodachrome 25   f4, 1/250

Another of the 15 preserved Stanier Class 5s which has returned to service is No 45428 which was built by Armstrong Whitworth in 1936. Following withdrawal in 1967 its new owners Brian Hollingsworth and G Drury based the locomotive at Tyseley, Birmingham, where on 3 May 1969 it was named *Eric Treacy* by the Bishop of Birmingham, after the eminent railway photographer Bishop Treacy. Since then No 45428 has been transferred to the NYMR and following a long period of inactivity awaiting repairs has now been returned to service and looks very smart in BR lined black livery as it passes Moorgates with a train from Grosmont to Pickering. 12 August 1984. *(David Peaker)*
Mamiya 645   80mm Sekor
Fujichrome 100   f5.6, 1/500

The evening sun bathes Class 5 No 44767 *George Stephenson* as it draws away southwards from Stirling returning to Falkirk after a visit to the BR open day at Perth. 13 April 1985. (L A Nixon)

Pentax SP   85mm Takumar
Kodachrome 64   f4.5, 1/250

The highly-scenic Settle & Carlisle line which runs along part of the Pennines, the 'Backbone of England', is not all mountain and moorland scenery. North of Appleby the railway comes down into quite different pastoral and wooded countryside as it follows the course of the River Eden towards Carlisle. On a very warm and sunny day over the Spring Bank Holiday weekend the pairing of two Stanier 4-6-0 types, Class 5 No 5407 piloting Class 5XP No 5690 *Leander*, took place and they are seen in a pleasant setting at Culgaith as they head north with the 'Cumbrian Mountain Express'. 29 May 1982. *(Hugh Ballantyne)*
Leica M4-2   90mm f4 Elmarit
Kodachrome 25   f4, 1/250

The setting sun of a late autumn day glinting off 'Princess Coronation' Class No 46229 *Duchess of Hamilton* turns the big Stanier Pacific into a 'Golden Duchess' as she slows for the water stop at Garsdale whilst working a southbound 'Cumbrian Mountain Pullman'. 8 November 1980. *(David C Rodgers)*
Pentax K1000   50mm Takumar
Kodachrome 25   f2.8, 1/250

The SVR's own Ivatt Class 2F No 46443, together with other SVR engines, was an important participant in the 'GWR 150' events which took place during 1985. Though in no way a GWR locomotive, there was a precedent for using this pure LMS design in those celebrations as the last 25 of the 128 engines in the class were built at Swindon in 1952-53 and some were used on the Western Region, particularly on former Cambrian lines in Wales. During the 'GWR 150' season, No 46443 broke new ground by being used on the now closed Portishead branch and also ran some trains along the Bristol Harbour line. In this picture it is seen leaving the majestic station of Bristol Temple Meads with one of the Portishead trains. 2 June 1985. *(John Kenward)*
Canon AE-1 Program
Ektachrome 100   f5.6, 1/500